Fanny Snow Knowlton

Nature Songs for Children

Fanny Snow Knowlton

Nature Songs for Children

ISBN/EAN: 9783744775083

Printed in Europe, USA, Canada, Australia, Japan

Cover: Foto ©Thomas Meinert / pixelio.de

More available books at **www.hansebooks.com**

NATURE SONGS

FOR CHILDREN.

FANNY SNOW KNOWLTON.

There is ever a song somewhere my dear,
There is ever a something sings alway.
Riley.

1917
MILTON BRADLEY COMPANY,
Springfield, Mass.
NEW YORK.   PHILADELPHIA.   ATLANTA.   SAN FRANCISCO.

To my little boy
DONALD
My critic, counselor and most
appreciative listener these songs are
lovingly inscribed by his
MOTHER.

TABLE OF CONTENTS.

THE MONTHS.

January,	Christina G. Rossetti, 6	July,	Frank Dempster Sherman, 17
February,	Lisbeth B. Comins, 8	August,	Anna M. Pratt, 18
March,	G. W. W. Houghton, 10	September,	Helen Hunt Jackson, 19
April,	Phœbe Cary, 12	October,	Anna M. Pratt, 21
May,	Anna M. Pratt, 14	November,	Clinton Scollard, 22
Oh, the Merry Lay of June,	Augusta Davis Webster, 16	December,	Laura E. Richards, 24

FLOWER SONGS.

Pussy Willow,	· · · · · 28	Dandelion,	· · · · · · 32
A Pinky Wild Rose,	Anna M. Pratt, 29	Daisy Nurses,	· · · · · · 33
The Crocus,	Belle Willey Gue, 30	Calling the Violet,	Lucy Larcom, 34
The Dandelion Cycle,	Emilie Poulsson, 30	Clovers,	Helena Leeming Jelliffe, 36

BIRD SONGS.

What Robin Told,	George Cooper, 38	Three Little Doves,	James Johonnot, 44
The Call of the Crow,	Margaret E. Sangster, 40	The Captive Bird,	Emily Huntington Miller, 46
The Snowbird,	Frank Dempster Sherman, 42	Rollicking Robin,	Lucy Larcom, 48

GAMES.

Points of the Compass,	Anna M. Pratt, 52	The Scissors Grinder,	L. A. France, 60
Ten Little Ponies,	Malana A. Harris, 54	Game to teach Five,	Jessie Norton, 62
The Postman,	Anna M. Pratt, 56	Snowballs,	Esther Anna Godwin, 63
Game with First Kindergarten Gift,	Malana A. Harris, 57	A Family Drum Corps, Sow, Sew, So,	Malcolm Douglas, 64 Eva Lovett Carson, 66
Out of the Window,	Jessie Norton, 58	Over in the Meadow,	Olive A. Wadsworth, 68
Feeding the Chickens,	Anna M. Pratt, 59		

MISCELLANEOUS.

Little Bo-Peep,	Amanda Stout, 70	The Ripened Leaves,	Margaret E. Sangster, 81
Sequel to an old Story,	Emilie Poulsson, 72	A Day,	Emily Dickinson, 82
A Little Fairy,	Margaret E. Sangster, 74	It is Spring,	Celia Thaxter, 84
Afternoon Tea,	Mary F. Butts, 75	An April Rain,	Dora Read Goodale, 86
Kite Time,	Jessie B Sherman, 76	A Summer Shower,	Sydney Dayre, 88
Little Friends,	Anna M. Pratt, 77	June Roses,	Belle Willey Gue, 91
Little Hickory Nut,	Elizabeth H. Thomas, 78	In the Tree-top,	Lucy Larcom, 94
North and South,	Anna M. Pratt, 79	The Merry Wind,	Margaret E. Sangster, 96
News for Gardeners,	Anna M. Pratt, 80		

SACRED SONGS.

Morning Prayer,	Malana A. Harris, 100	God loves His Little Children,	Anna M. Pratt, 104
Now the Day is over,	· · · 101	Hymn for National Holiday,	Margaret E. Sangster, 105
Patriotic Hymn,	Margaret E. Sangster, 102	Merry Bells of Easter,	· · · · 106
Litany,	Margaret E. Sangster, 103	A Hymn for a Child,	Laura E. Richards, 108

THE MONTHS.

Said the Child to the youthful Year:
  "What hast thou in store for me,
O giver of beautiful gifts, what cheer,
  What joy dost thou bring with thee?"

"My seasons four shall bring
  Their treasures: the winter's snows,
The autumn's store, and the flowers of spring,
  And the summer's perfect rose."
CELIA THAXTER.

JANUARY.

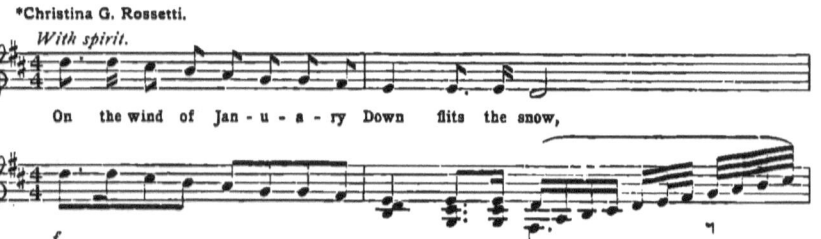

* By permission of ROBERT BROTHERS, publishers.

JANUARY.

FEBRUARY.

* From "Our Little Ones," and the "Nursery," by permission of Estes & Lauriat, Publishers.

FEBRUARY.

MARCH.

MAY.

*Anna. M. Pratt

1. The or-chard is a ro-sy cloud, The oak a ro-sy mist, And
2. A mes-sage comes a-cross the fields, Born on the balm-y air; For

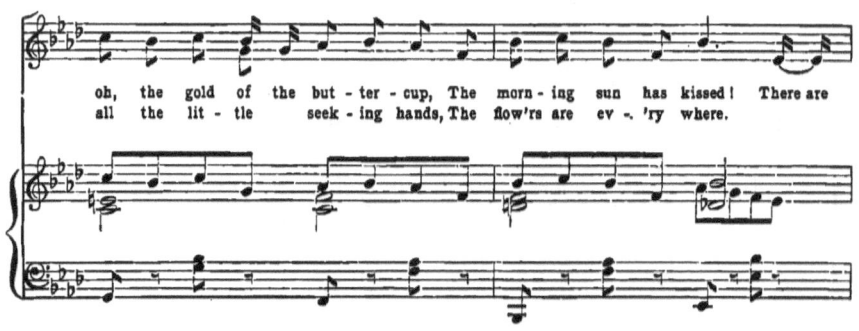

oh, the gold of the but-ter-cup, The morn-ing sun has kissed! There are
all the lit-tle seek-ing hands, The flow'rs are ev-'ry where.

twink-ling shad-ows on the grass, Of a myr-iad ti-ny leaves, And a
Hark! a mur-m'ring in the hive; List a car-ol sweet; While

* From "St. Nicholas," by permission of THE CENTURY CO., Publishers.

MAY.

OH, THE MERRY LAY OF JUNE.

Augusta Davies Webster.

(16)

JULY.

*Frank Dempster Sherman.

July, for you the songs are sung By birds the leafy trees among: July, for you in silence deep, The world seems fallen fast asleep. Save on one glorious holiday, When all our books we put away, And ev'ry little maid and man Is proud to be American.

*By permission of and arrangement with Messrs Houghton Mifflin & Co., publishers of Mr. Sherman's "Little Folk Lyrics."

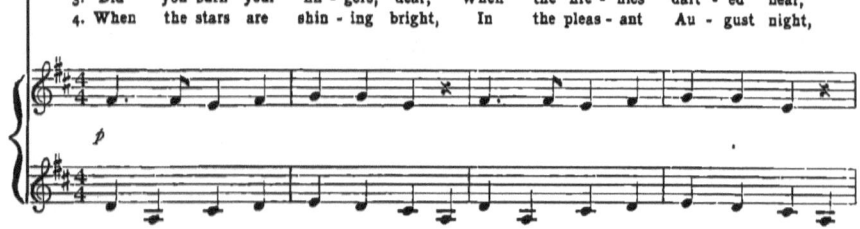
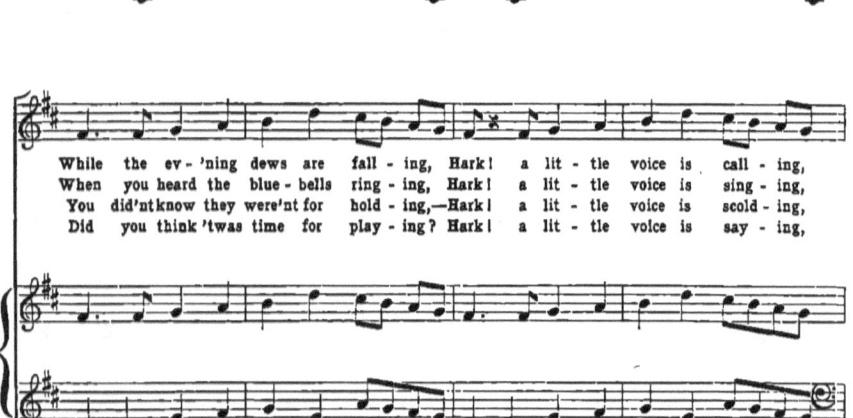

SEPTEMBER.

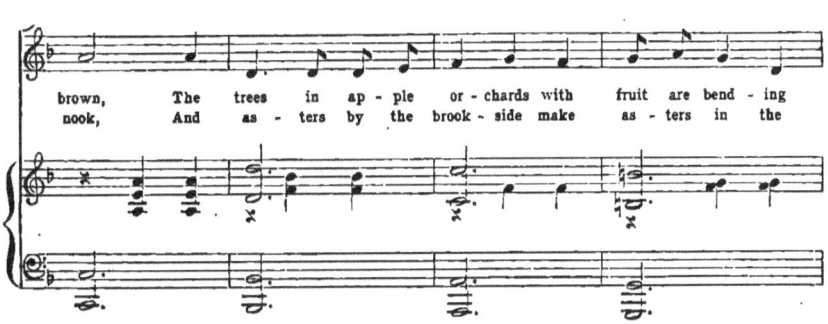

SEPTEMBER.

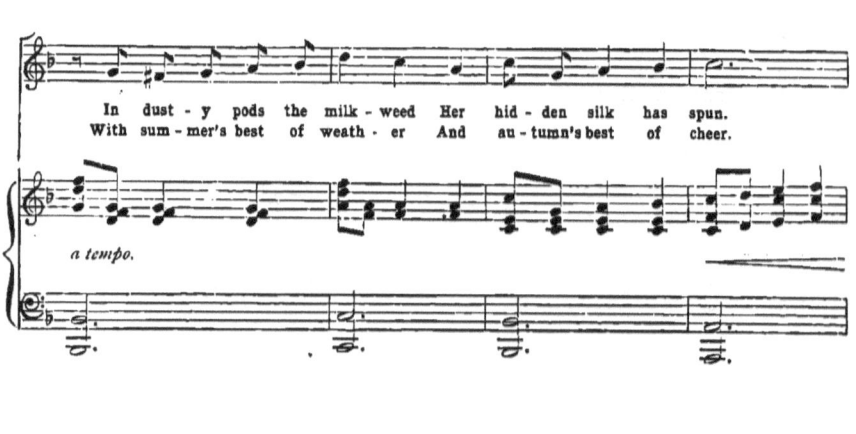

In dust-y pods the milk-weed Her hid-den silk has spun.
With sum-mer's best of weath-er And au-tumn's best of cheer.

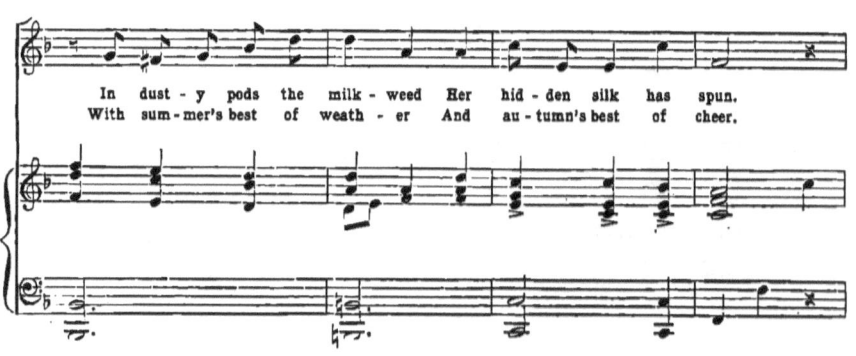

In dust-y pods the milk-weed Her hid-den silk has spun.
With sum-mer's best of weath-er And au-tumn's best of cheer.

NOVEMBER.

*Clinton Scollard.

1. Wide o'er the wold, Through field and fold,
2. No blos-soms bright Of red and white
3. But why re-pine, O heart of mine?

Sempre legato.

The wind moans cold, And sighs in sad-ness;
Set sweet de-light Of fra-grance float-ing;
Joy still is thine, Though days grow cold-er;

The dream-y days Have gone their ways,
All that was fair Is bleak and bare;
And snows will bring, In fra-grant spring,

* By permission of the Author.

(22)

NOVEMBER.

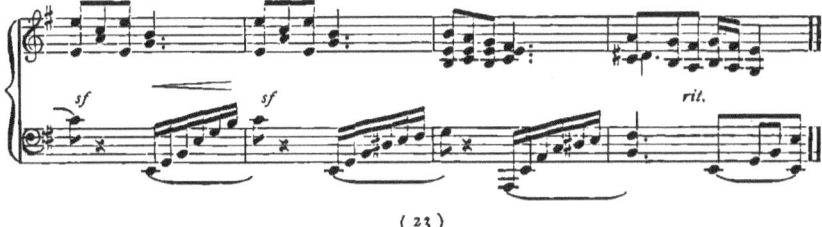

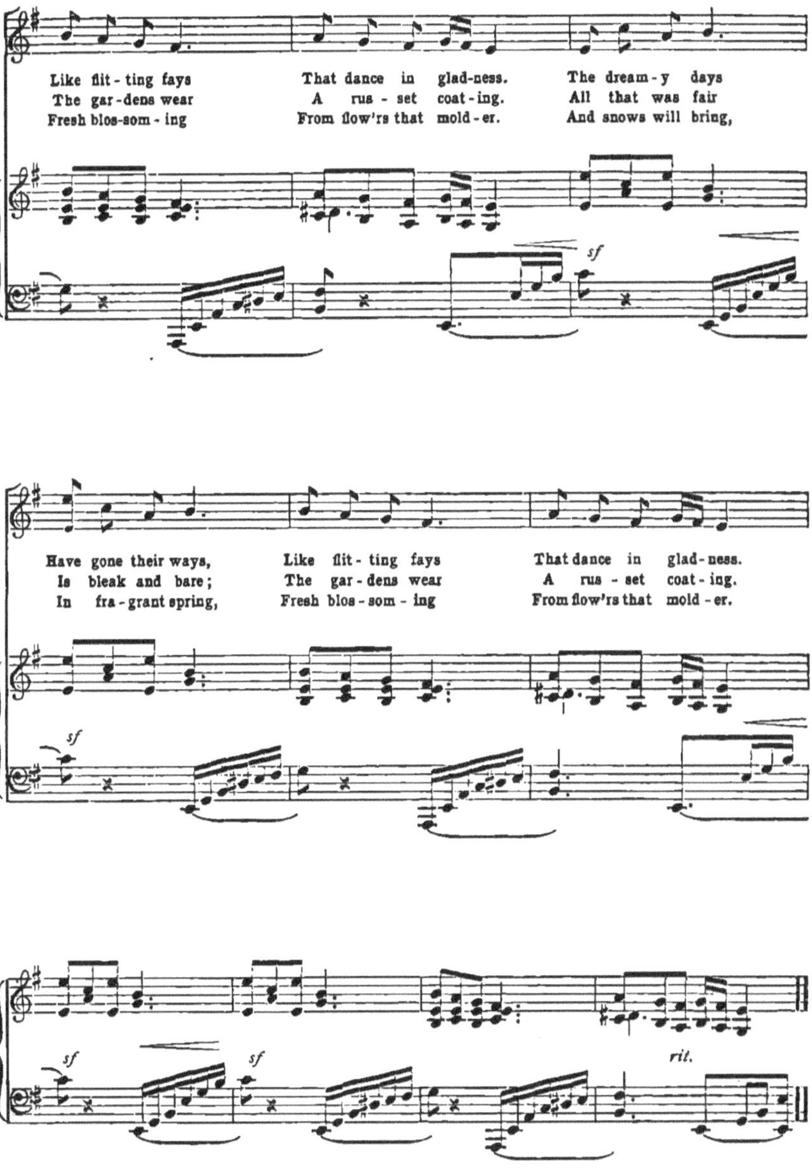
Like flit - ting fays That dance in glad-ness. The dream - y days
The gar - dens wear A rus - set coat - ing. All that was fair
Fresh blos-som - ing From flow'rs that mold - er. And snows will bring,
sf
sf
Have gone their ways, Like flit - ting fays That dance in glad - ness.
Is bleak and bare; The gar - dens wear A rus - set coat - ing.
In fra - grant spring, Fresh blos - som - ing From flow'rs that mold - er.
sf
sf
rit.

DECEMBER.

FLOWER SONGS.

"Sing, sing, lily bells ring,
 The blossoms are coming to town,
Dasies and lilies and daffy-down-dillies
 Each in a sweet new gown."

PUSSY WILLOW.

PUSSY WILLOW.

A PINKY WILD ROSE.
(CRADLE SONG.)
Anna M. Pratt.

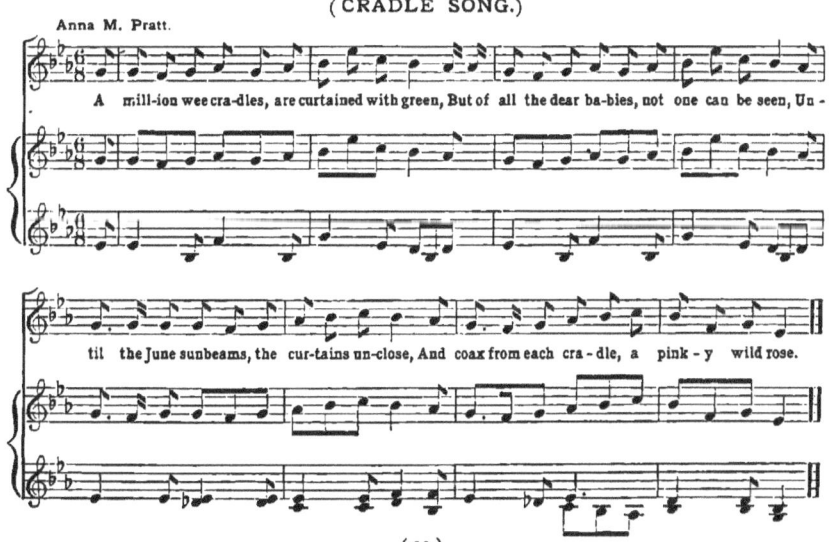

THE CROCUS.

Belle Willey Gue.
Moderato.

1. Brave lit - tle cro - - cus, what's in your cup?
2. Are you not hun - - gry, lone - ly and cold?
3. Bright, cheer - y cro - - cus, we wish you'd stay;

Smooth.

Staccato.

Snow - flakes and sun - beams I've gath - ered up.
Snow - flakes sus - tain me, sun - beams en - fold.
Oth - er flow'rs fol - low; I'll haste a - way.

THE DANDELION CYCLE.

*Emilie Poulsson.

1. Pret - ty lit - tle Gol - di - locks, shin - ing in the sun,
2. And where rests a sil - ver hair that has blown from me,

* From "In The Child's World," by permission of MILTON BRADLEY Co., Publisher.

THE DANDELION CYCLE.

DANDELION.

From "Little Flower Folks," by permission of the EDUCATIONAL PUBLISHING CO.

CALLING THE VIOLET.

*Lucy Larcom.

* By permission of and arrangement with Messrs Houghton Mifflin & Co., publishers of Lucy Larcom's poems.

CALLING THE VIOLET.

CLOVERS.

*Words from the "Outlook" by permission.

BIRD SONGS.

"So the merry brown thrush sings away in the tree,
 To you and to me, to you and to me;
 And he sings all the day, little girl, little boy
  Oh, the world's running over with joy."
                            LUCY LARCOM.

WHAT ROBIN TOLD.

THE CALL OF THE CROW.

*Margaret E. Sangster.

* From "Little Knights and Ladies." Copyright, 1895, by HARPER & BROS.

THE CALL OF THE CROW.

THE SNOWBIRD.

Frank Dempster Sherman.

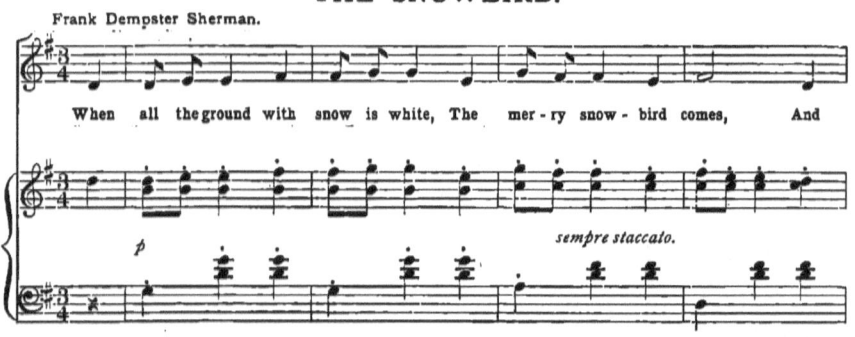

When all the ground with snow is white, The mer-ry snow-bird comes, And

hops a-bout with great de-light, To find the scat-tered crumbs. How

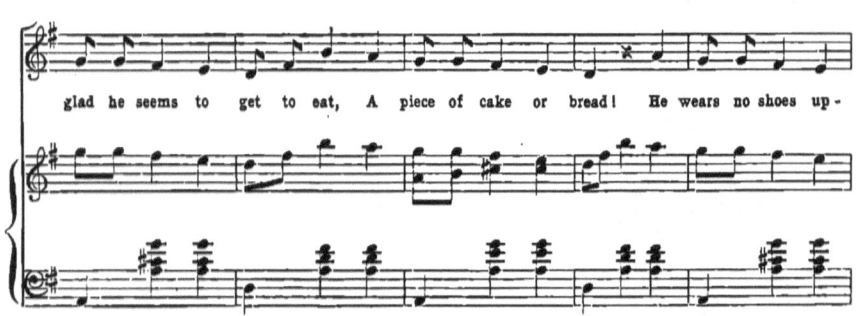

glad he seems to get to eat, A piece of cake or bread! He wears no shoes up-

By permission of, and arrangement with, Messrs. Houghton, Mifflin & Co., publishers of Mr. Sherman's "Little Folk Lyrics."

THE SNOWBIRD.

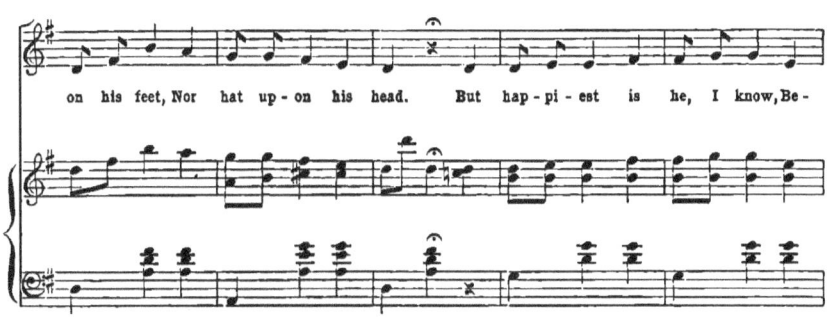

THREE LITTLE DOVES.

James Johonnot.

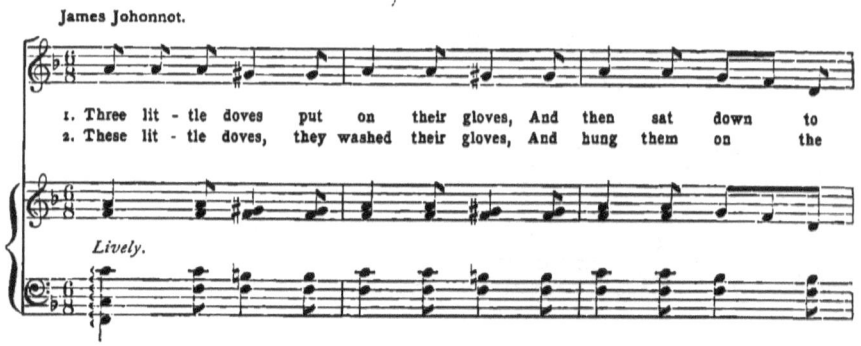

1. Three lit - tle doves put on their gloves, And then sat down to
2. These lit - tle doves, they washed their gloves, And hung them on the

Lively.

dine. . . . These lit - tle doves, they soiled their gloves, And soon were heard to
line. . . . These lit - tle doves, they dried their gloves, And thought it ver - y

whine, "Oh moth - er dear, come here, come here, . .
fine. . . "Oh moth - er dear, come here, come here, . .

THREE LITTLE DOVES.

THE CAPTIVE BIRD.

* By permission.

THE CAPTIVE BIRD.

ROLLICKING ROBIN.

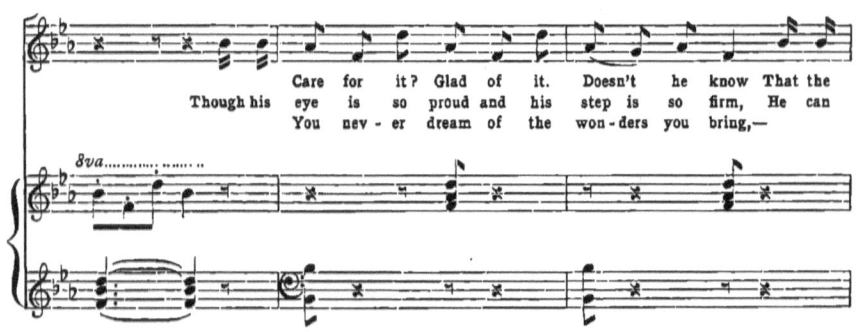

*By permission of and arrangement with Messrs. Houghton, Mifflin & Co., publishers of Lucy Larcom's poems.

ROLLICKING ROBIN.

ROLLICKING ROBIN.

GAMES.

"The world is so full of a number of things,
I'm sure we should all be as happy as kings."
R. L. STEVENSON.

POINTS OF THE COMPASS.

POINTS OF THE COMPASS.

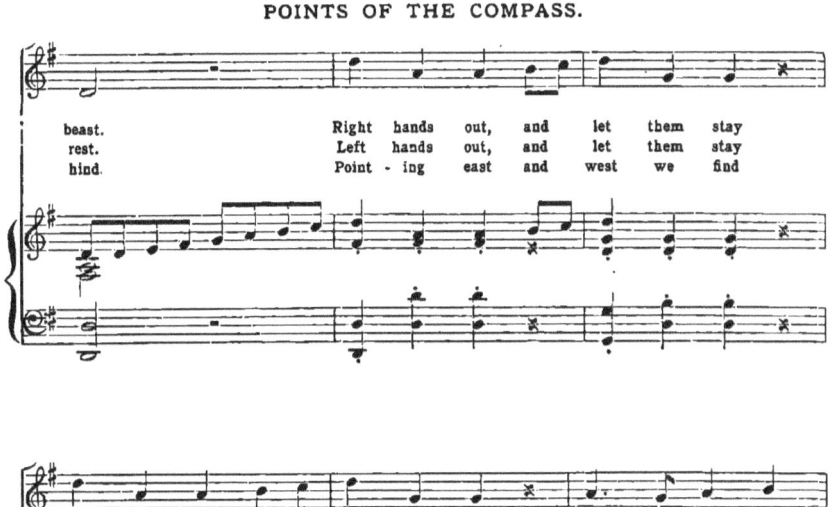

TEN LITTLE PONIES.
(FINGER PLAY.)

1. Ten little po - nies, read - y for a
2. Five touch'd by fair - ies, now are lit - tle
3. Now touch of fair - ies turn the five to

race, Each of them go - - ing
boys, All fond of frol - - ic,
girls, Play they are dol - - lies,

at a gen - tle pace; Now they are
full of play - ful joys; All fond of
with some gold - en curls; Take dol - lies

TEN LITTLE PONIES.

trot - - ting, now how fast they run,
play - - ing, skip - ping all a - round,
rid - - ing in a char - iot fine,

See, fast - er, fast - er, oh, it is such fun!
Boys nev - er hap - pier, an - y - where are found.
Five po - nies lead - ing; what a hap - py time.

THE POSTMAN.

GAME WITH FIRST KINDERGARTEN GIFT.*

Malana A. Harris.

1. My ball will be an ap-ple red; 'Tis hang-ing on a tree. The
2. My ball will be an or-ange round, Just from the sun-ny south. So
3. Mine is the gold-en pen-du-lum That swings with-in the clock; That

wind will shake the branch-es now, And throw it down to me.
fra-grant, nice, and jui-cy too, To put with-in my mouth.
tells the time of day to us, And al-ways says "tick tock."

4 My ball is a tomato green,
   Low hanging on the vine;
   And when the sunshine paints it red,
   It surely will be mine.

5 Mine is a little birdie blue,
   To place within a nest.
   It has been hopping all around,
   And now it wants to rest.

6 My ball I call a purple plum,
   About as large as papa's thumb.
   Inside there is a pit for me,
   To plant that it may grow a tree.

7 We'll put them all together now,
   And look at them again;
   They're something like the rainbow bright.
   That we saw through the rain.

1st verse, red ball; 2nd verse, orange ball; 3rd verse, yellow ball; 4th verse, green ball; 5th verse, blue ball; 6th, purple ball; 7th verse, all together.

THE SCISSORS GRINDER.

From "Our Little Ones" and the "Nursery," by permission of Estes & Lauriat, publishers.

THE SCISSORS GRINDER.

GAME TO TEACH FIVE.

By permission of THE BURROWS BROTHERS Co., publishers.

SNOWBALLS.

A FAMILY DRUM CORPS.

* From "St. Nicholas," by permission of The Century Co.

A FAMILY DRUM CORPS.

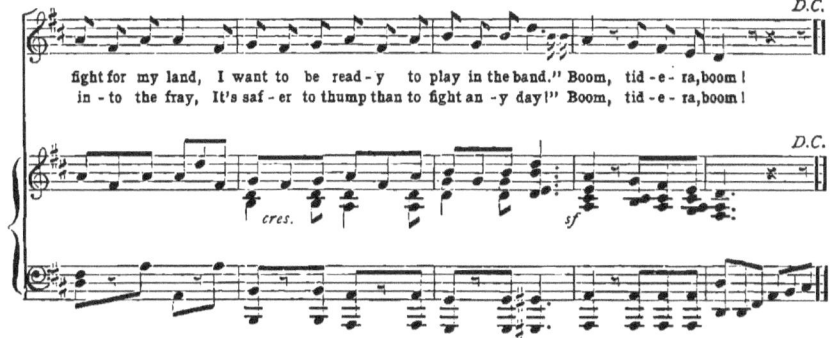

3 And showing her spirit, the little man's wife,
　Boom, tidera, boom!
With some of her pin-money purchased a fife,
　Boom, tidera, boom!
And picking out tunes that were not very hard,
They'd play them while marching around the back yard,
Without for one's feelings the slightest regard,
　Boom, tidera, boom!

4 The little old parson, who lived next door,
　Boom, tidera, boom!
Would throw up his hands as he walked the floor,
　Boom, tidera, boom!
"Won't you stop it, I beg you?" he often said;
"I'm trying to think of a text, but instead
The only thing I can get into my head
　Is your boom, tidera, boom!"

5 And all of the people for miles around,
　Boom, tidera, boom!
Kept time at their tasks to the martial sound,
　Boom, tidera, boom!
While children to windows and stoops would fly,
Expecting to see a procession pass by,
And they couldn't make out why it never drew nigh,
　With its boom, tidera, boom!

6 It would seem that such vigor must soon abate
　Boom, tidera, boom!
But still they keep at it, early and late,
　Boom, tidera, boom!
So, if it should be that a war breaks out,
They'll all be ready, I have no doubt,
To help in putting the foe to rout,
　With their boom, tidera, boom!

OVER IN THE MEADOW.

MISCELLANEOUS.

"How the heart of childhood dances
 Upon a sunny day:
It has its own romances,
 And a wide, wide world have they."
                    L. E. LANDON.

LITTLE BO-PEEP.

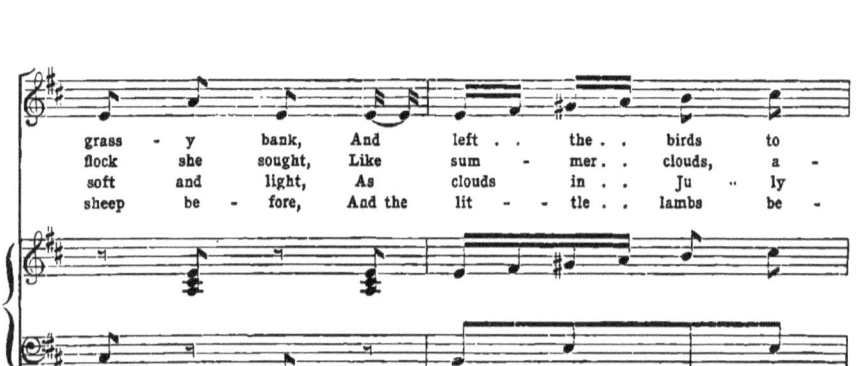

LITTLE BO-PEEP.

SEQUEL TO AN OLD STORY.

Emilie Poulsson.

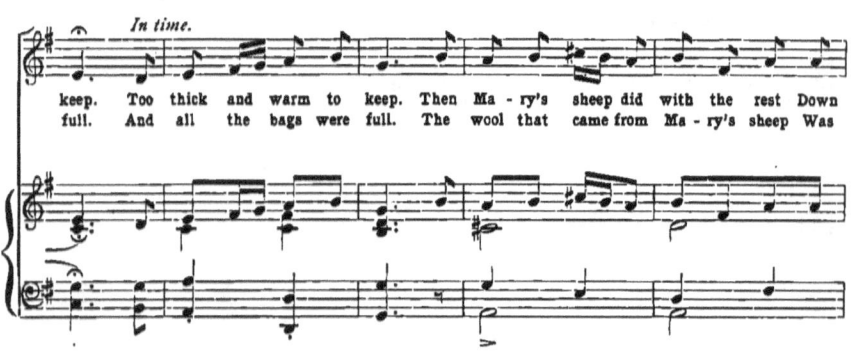

* From "In The Child's World," by permission of Milton Bradley Co., Publishers.

SEQUEL TO AN OLD STORY.

A LITTLE FAIRY.

*Margaret E. Sangster.

* From "Little Knights and Ladies." Copyright, 1895, by Harper & Bros.

AFTERNOON TEA.

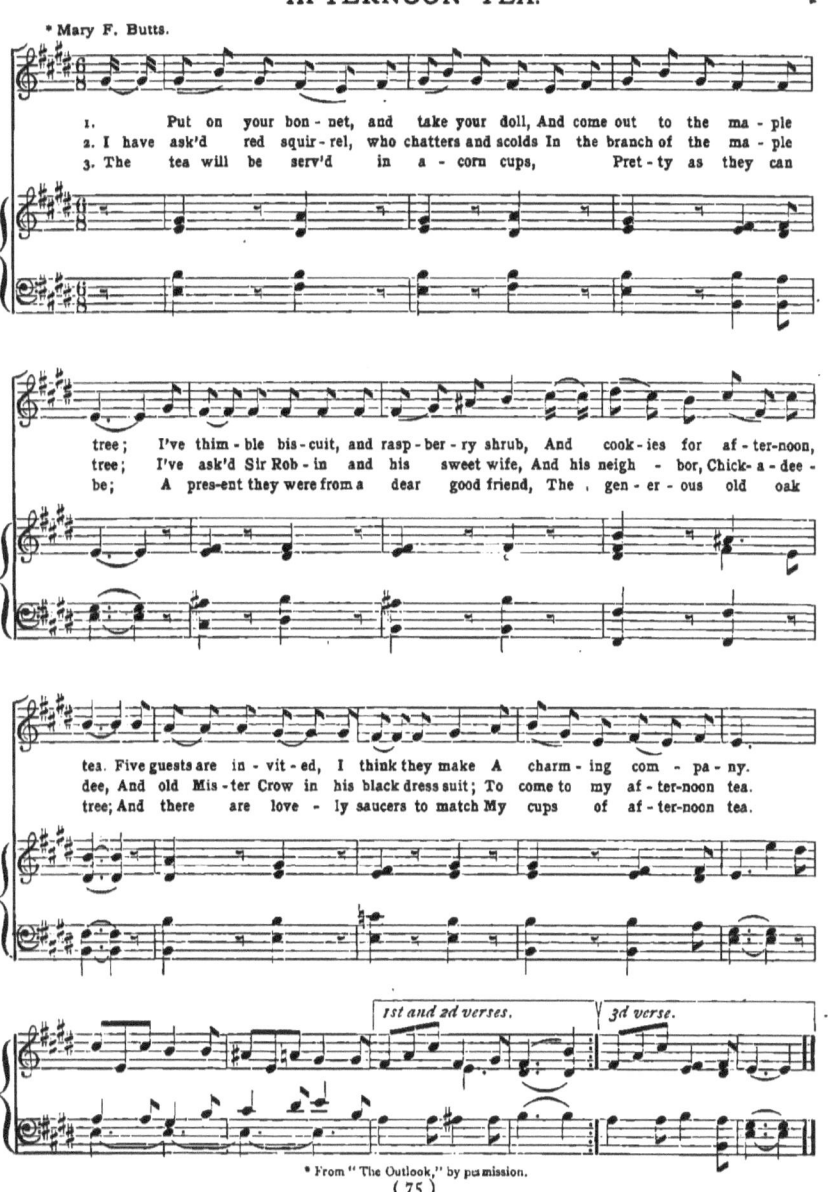

* From "The Outlook," by permission.

LITTLE FRIENDS.

*From "Youth's Companion," by permission.

LITTLE HICKORY NUT.

*Elizabeth H. Thomas.

* From "Youth's Companion," by permission.

LITTLE HICKORY NUT.

NORTH AND SOUTH.

*Anna M. Pratt.

* From "Youth's Companion," by permission.

NEWS FOR GARDENERS.

From "Youth's Companion," by permission.

THE RIPENED LEAVES.

A DAY.

* By permission of ROBERTS BROTHERS, Publishers.

A DAY.

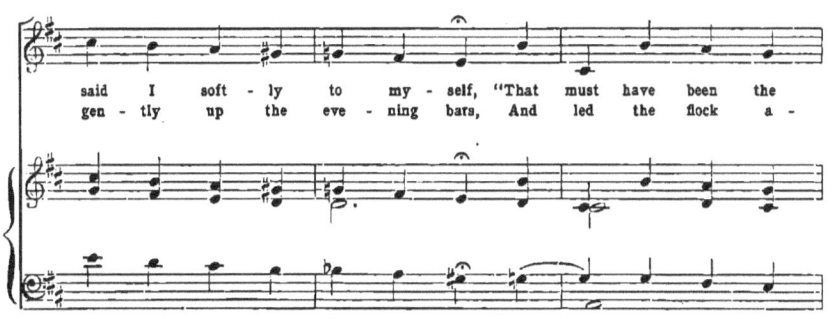

IT IS SPRING.
(WILD GEESE.)

* By permission of and arrangement with Messrs. Houghton, Mifflin & Co., publishers of Celia Thaxter's poems.

IT IS SPRING.

AN APRIL RAIN.

*Dora Read Goodale.

* From "Apple Blossoms," by permission of G. P. Putnam's Sons, publishers.

AN APRIL RAIN.

A SUMMER SHOWER.

*From "Youth's Companion," by permission.

A SUMMER SHOWER.

A SUMMER SHOWER.

JUNE ROSES.

JUNE ROSES.

JUNE ROSES.

IN THE TREE-TOP.

THE MERRY WIND.

*Margaret E. Sangster.

*From "Little Knights and Ladies." Copyright, 1895, by Harper Brothers.

THE MERRY WIND.

THE MERRY WIND.

SACRED SONGS.

"Suffer little children
To come unto me."

MORNING PRAYER.

Malana A. Harris.

1. We thank Thee dear Fa - ther, For care through the night, For flow - ers that blos - som In morn - ing's clear light.
2. For wind, rain, and sun - shine, For home, friends, and food, From Thee comes each bless - ing, And ev - 'ry - thing good.
3. Our Fa - ther in heav - en, Be with us each

MORNING PRAYER.

NOW THE DAY IS OVER.

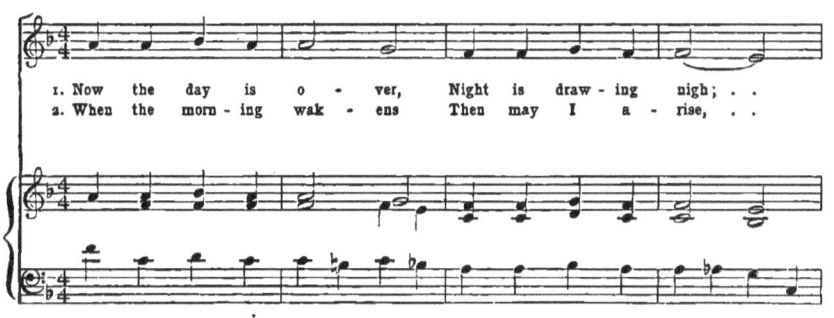

PATRIOTIC HYMN.

*From "Little Knights and Ladies." Copyright, 1895, by HARPER AND BROTHERS.

PATRIOTIC HYMN.

LITANY.

*Margaret E. Sangster.
Cheerfully.

1. Chil - dren, sing to Him whose love Broods our hap - py lives a - bove.
2. For the flow'rs and for the wheat, For the cold and for the heat,
3. For the moth - er's look of grace, For the ba - by's lit - tle face,

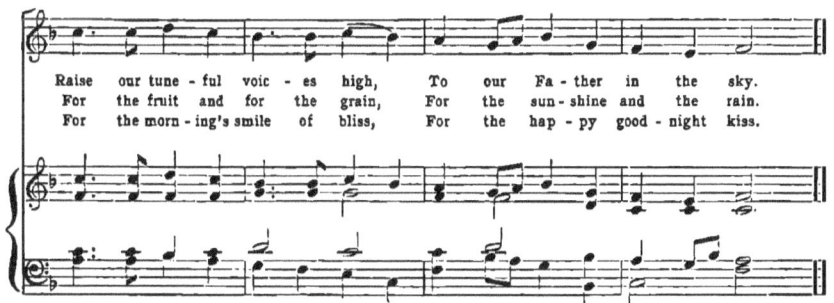

Raise our tune - ful voic - es high, To our Fa - ther in the sky.
For the fruit and for the grain, For the sun - shine and the rain.
For the morn - ing's smile of bliss, For the hap - py good - night kiss.

* From "Little Knights and Ladies." Copyright, 1895, by HARPER & BROS.

GOD LOVES HIS LITTLE CHILDREN.

(104)

GOD LOVES HIS LITTLE CHILDREN.

HYMN FOR NATIONAL HOLIDAY.

*Margaret E. Sangster.

*From "Little Knights and Ladies." Copyright, 1895, by Harper & Bros.

MERRY BELLS OF EASTER.
(SPRING LIFE.)

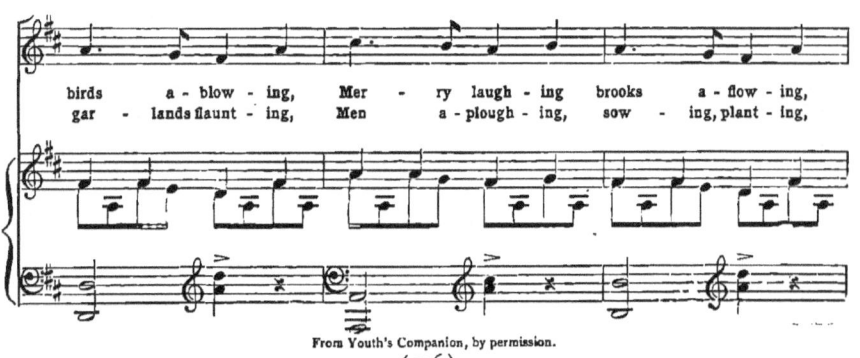

From Youth's Companion, by permission.

MERRY BELLS OF EASTER.

A HYMN FOR A CHILD.

From Youth's Companion, by permission.

INDEX OF FIRST LINES.

	PAGE
Ah, the drops are falling down	88
A little brown baby, so round and so wee	78
A little man bought him a big brass drum	64
A million wee cradles are curtained with green	29
Birdie, up in your cage so gay	46
Brave little crocus, what's in your cup?	30
Caw, Caw, Caw	40
Children sing to Him whose love	103
Come up, April, through the valley	12
Dandelion, Dandelion, Where's your cap of gold?	32
Dear little violet, Don't be afraid	34
Ev'ry day the shining sun	52
For all the pleasant things I see	108
For peace and for plenty	102
Good morning, Mister Postman	56
Hark the sky-lark in the cloud	16
How do robins build their nest?	38
I'll tell you how the sun rose	82
In March come the March winds	10
In the pleasant August night	18
July, for you the songs are sung	17
June roses are fairies, imprisoned but happy	91

	PAGE
Let us sing to Him whose hand	105
Little snowflakes falling lightly	77
Mary had a little lamb, Which grew to be a sheep	72
Merry bells of Easter ring	106
Merry Christmas; Merry Christmas	24
My ball will be an apple red	57
North winds do blow	76
Now the day is over	101
Oh, I'm a scissors grinder	60
One little cat in the corner	62
On the wind of January, Down flits the snow	6
Out of the window, over the way	58
Over in the meadow, in the sand, in the sun	68
Pretty little Goldilocks, shining in the sun	30
Put on your bonnet and take your doll	75
Rock-a-by, baby, up in the tree-top	94
Rollicking Robin is here again	48
Said the leaves upon the branches, One sunny autumn day	81
Snow-balls, snow-balls, Oh, such jolly fun	63
Ten little ponies, ready for a race	54
The brook is brimmed with melting snow	28
The clovers have no time to play	36

INDEX OF FIRST LINES.

	PAGE
The daisies white are nursery maids, With frills upon their caps	33
The drops are falling, falling	86
The elm and the maple, the ash and the oak	21
The goldenrod is yellow	19
The little boys in Labrador	79
The merry wind came racing	96
The orchard is a rosy cloud	14
The wind blows, the sun shines, the birds sing loud	84
There was a little gardener, Who spent the summer days	80
Three little doves put on their gloves	44
This is the way my father sows, As up and down the field he goes	66
We have a little fairy, Who flits about the house	74
We'll mix up some water and meal in a pan	59
We thank Thee, dear Father	100
When all the ground with snow is white	42
When I go to sleep at night	104
When little Bo Peep had lost her sheep	70
Who can this little maiden be?	8
Wide o'er the wold, Through field and fold	22

www.ingramcontent.com/pod-product-compliance
Lightning Source LLC
Chambersburg PA
CBHW020144170426
43199CB00010B/887